Searchlight
BOOKS™

What
Are Energy
Sources?

Finding Out about

Solar

Energy

Matt Doeden

Lerner Publications Company
Minneapolis

Lerner Publications Company
A division of Lerner Publishing Group, Inc.
241 First Avenue North
Minneapolis, MN 55401 USA

For reading levels and more information, look up this title at www.lernerbooks.com.

Library of Congress Cataloging-in-Publication Data

Doeden, Matt, author.
        Finding out about solar energy / by Matt Doeden.
            pages   cm. — (Searchlight books™. What are energy sources?)
        Includes index.
        ISBN 978-1-4677-3657-2 (lib bdg. : alk. paper)
        ISBN 978-1-4677-4641-0 (eBook)
        1. Solar energy—Juvenile literature. 2. Renewable energy sources—Juvenile
    literature. I. Title.
    TJ810.3.D64 2015
    333.792'3—dc23   2013048329

Manufactured in the United States of America
1 — BP — 7/15/14

Contents

Chapter 1

WHAT IS SOLAR ENERGY?

Imagine yourself on the beach. It's a hot, bright summer day. You spread sunblock on your skin so you don't get a sunburn. Then you step off your beach towel. The sand is so hot that it almost hurts to walk on it. Time for a swim!

The sun bathes beaches with light and heat. What do we call power from the sun?

All that heat and light is coming from the sun's rays. The sun bathes Earth in free energy every second of every day. We can collect and use the sun's power. Power from the sun is called solar energy.

Solar energy is powerful and plentiful.

Where Does Solar Energy Come From?

The sun is made up of mostly hydrogen and helium. These are the two most common elements in the universe. The center of the sun is called the core. That's where the sun's power comes from. The core is like one giant power plant.

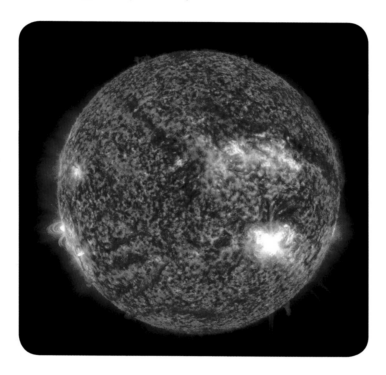

THE SUN'S POWER COMES FROM ITS CENTER, OR CORE.

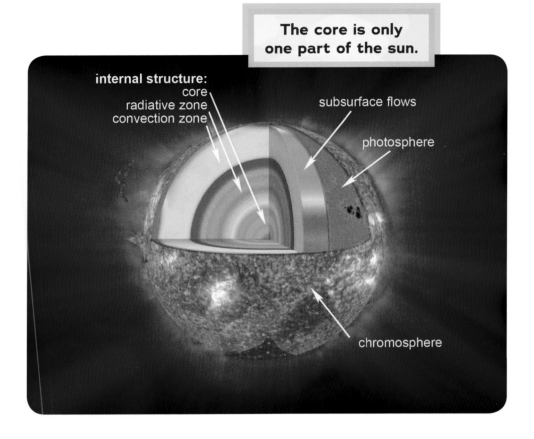

internal structure:
core
radiative zone
convection zone

subsurface flows

photosphere

chromosphere

In the sun's core, the temperature is more than
27,000,000°F (15,000,000°C). Gravity pulls much of the
hydrogen that makes up the sun deep into the sun's core.
This creates a huge amount of heat and pressure. The
heat and pressure cause two hydrogen atoms to join, or
fuse together. When that happens, the hydrogen atoms
form a single helium atom. That's where the helium in the
sun comes from. This is called nuclear fusion.

The new helium atom doesn't quite use all the mass of the two hydrogen atoms. There is a little left over. This mass is converted into energy—a *lot* of energy.

All the sun's energy comes from nuclear fusion.

The energy makes its way to the surface of the sun. The energy goes off into space as electromagnetic radiation. This type of energy includes light, X-rays, and more. Some of that energy hits Earth. This energy warms our planet, provides food for plants, and can be collected and used by people.

Plants rely on sunlight to make their own food.

Where Can We Collect Solar Energy?

We can collect solar energy anywhere the sun shines. But some places are better than others. Places that don't get much cloud cover are ideal. The sun shines brightly almost all the time in most deserts. They can be great places to collect solar power.

The desert is an excellent place to collect solar power.

This solar plant is in the Mojave Desert in California.

But there's a problem. Not many people live in deserts. It doesn't do much good to collect power if no one is there to use it. So the trick is to find sunny spots close to cities and towns. California's Mojave Desert is a perfect example. Lots of people live near it. That's why many solar power plants have been built there.

Chapter 2

COLLECTING SOLAR ENERGY

We can turn the sun's rays into electricity in several ways. Some methods work great on small scales, such as in a solar-powered calculator. Other ways, such as focusing the sun's rays to create very high temperatures, work best in large power plants.

Some calculators run on solar power. What is one way to collect solar power?

Photovoltaic Cells

One of the easiest ways to get power from the sun is through photovoltaic cells, or solar cells. In the word *photovoltaic*, *photo* means "light," and *voltaic* means "electricity." Solar cells turn sunlight into electricity.

This picture shows photovoltaic cells.

How do solar cells work? They are made of a material called a semiconductor. When light passes through the cell, this material absorbs some of the light's energy. The energy causes atoms to lose tiny particles called electrons. The electrons flow in one direction as an electric current. Then we get electricity!

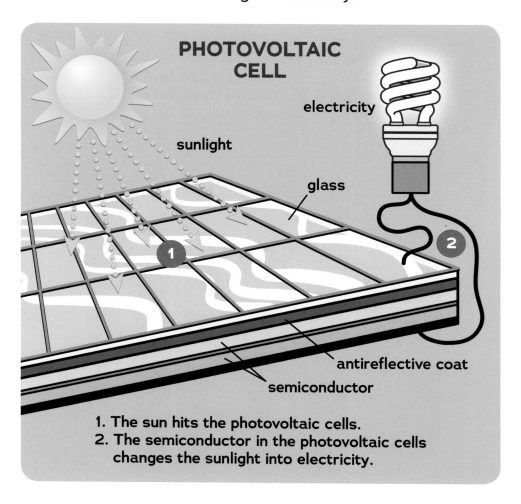

PHOTOVOLTAIC CELL

electricity

sunlight

glass

1

2

antireflective coat

semiconductor

1. The sun hits the photovoltaic cells.
2. The semiconductor in the photovoltaic cells changes the sunlight into electricity.

Solar cells are combined in large groups to form solar panels. Solar panels can help power a home or a business. They can power road signs or lights. In solar power plants, many solar panels are arranged in a solar array. Large solar arrays can power hundreds or even thousands of homes.

A solar panel powers this traffic sign.

Solar Thermal Power

Another way of using the sun's rays to make energy is called solar thermal power, or concentrated solar power. There are several ways to use solar thermal power. They all use the same basic idea. Solar thermal power concentrates the sun's rays to create heat. That heat is used to create electricity.

The mirrors in this solar thermal power plant focus the sun's heat onto one spot. The heat is used to generate electricity.

Mirrors reflect sunlight on a clear day at this solar power tower.

One type of solar thermal system is the solar power tower. This type of system includes mirrors that all face a tall tower. The mirrors focus the sunlight onto the top of the tower. Inside the tower is a liquid. The reflected rays heat this liquid to very high temperatures.

This solar power tower turns the sun's heat into electricity.

The heat then turns the liquid into steam. The moving steam turns the blades on a machine called a turbine. The turbine is connected to a generator. The generator turns the energy from the turbine's spinning blades into electricity.

Parabolic troughs work in a similar way. Curved mirrors focus sunlight onto pipes containing a fluid. The fluid heats up and moves to a central collection area. The hot fluid produces steam that moves a turbine. The turbine powers a generator that produces electricity.

THESE MIRRORS ON A PARABOLIC TROUGH CAPTURE SUNLIGHT VERY EFFICIENTLY.

Solar Fuel

Solar energy can also help create fuel. One way to do this is to use sunlight to split water molecules. Each water molecule has two hydrogen atoms and one oxygen atom. Energy from the sun can be used to break the molecule into oxygen and hydrogen. The hydrogen can be used as a fuel.

Scientists are researching more ways to turn sunlight and water into fuel.

Solar fuels are a new technology and are still being researched. But some people hope these fuels will one day replace oil-based gasoline used in vehicles.

In the future, vehicles might run on solar fuel rather than gasoline.

Chapter 3

THE PROS AND CONS OF SOLAR ENERGY

Most of the world's energy comes from fossil fuels. These include coal, oil, and natural gas. But fossil fuels are nonrenewable. This means once they are gone, they are gone for good.

Fossil fuels are nonrenewable. What does *nonrenewable* mean?

Solar energy is renewable. We can collect it as long as the sun keeps shining. That's why many people believe it will become more and more important in the future.

SOLAR ENERGY MAY BE AN IMPORTANT SOLUTION TO OUR ENERGY NEEDS IN YEARS AHEAD.

The Environment

Burning fossil fuels releases a lot of carbon dioxide. Too much of this gas going into the atmosphere is causing Earth's climate to change. And too much change could be a disaster.

More severe droughts might be one effect of climate change.

Solar power is one of the cleanest energy sources in the world. It doesn't give off pollution or release any carbon dioxide. That makes it an excellent way to help slow climate change.

Solar power doesn't create pollution.

A worker wears protective clothing while working with solar panels.

Solar power does come with some risks. Chemicals are used during the manufacture of solar panels. And some solar panels contain toxic materials.

The toxic materials in solar panels do not pollute the air when the panels are in use. However, they could pose a danger if the panels are just thrown away. The toxic materials could leak into the ground and even into the water supply. That's why it's important to recycle and dispose of solar panels correctly.

Silicon is removed from old solar panels and reused in new panels.

Cost

Solar energy is very expensive. It can cost thousands of dollars to install solar panels on just one home. Eventually, people recover these costs through lower electricity bills. But the up-front cost still makes it difficult for many people to buy solar panels.

The up-front costs of solar power are high, but it can pay off in the long run.

As solar power becomes more affordable, more solar panels are springing up.

Solar power continues to become cheaper as technology improves. One day, it may become cheaper than fossil fuels.

Unreliable Energy

Another con of solar power is that it is unreliable. Solar panels and plants work best when the sun is shining brightly. They don't work as well when it's cloudy. And they don't produce electricity at night.

Solar panels are ineffective once the sun goes down.

Solar power can be stored in batteries like these, but it's very expensive.

Storing solar power is expensive. That means solar energy is likely to be only one piece of the energy puzzle. Other power sources will be used alongside solar energy.

Chapter 4

SOLAR ENERGY IN THE FUTURE

Fossil fuels are going to run out some day. And people are growing more worried about climate change. So the push for alternative energy sources is on.

Solar panels like these are becoming more common. What is one reason people are turning to alternative energy sources?

This "green" community is powered by the sun.

Solar power is leading the way. Solar cells are getting cheaper and more efficient with every passing year. Many new homes have solar panels built into their roofs. And more solar power plants are being built in the world's sunniest regions.

These turbines turn wind
energy into electricity.

The growth of solar power will likely continue. Many
people imagine a day when renewable energy sources
such as solar, wind, and hydropower can work together to
power the world.

Solar Power in Space

Think about some of the drawbacks of solar panels. They work only during daylight. They don't work well when it's cloudy. And they take up a lot of room. How could we solve all those problems? It's simple. Put a solar plant in space!

Overcast days pose a challenge to solar panels.

That idea is not just science fiction. Companies are researching how to put a solar plant in orbit around Earth or even on the moon. Such a solar plant would be very expensive to build. But solar plants in space could produce electricity almost nonstop. The energy could be beamed to Earth's surface using radio waves or lasers. It may sound like a wild idea. But one day, much of our solar power may come from space!

SOLAR PANELS MAY SOMEDAY BE ON THE MOON!

Solar power plays an important role in the quest for clean energy.

We don't know whether it will ever really happen. But one thing is likely. As long as the sun shines on Earth, solar power is going to be a big part of our energy future.

Glossary

alternative energy source: a source of energy other than traditional fossil fuels

array: a group of things forming a complete unit

atom: the smallest unit of an element that has the properties of the element. An atom is made up of protons, neutrons, and electrons.

core: the center of the sun, where nuclear fusion occurs

fossil fuel: a fuel such as coal, natural gas, or oil that was formed over millions of years from the remains of dead plants and animals

generator: a machine that turns mechanical energy into electricity

nonrenewable: not able to be replenished. Once a nonrenewable form of energy is gone, it is used up forever.

renewable: able to be replenished over time

semiconductor: a substance that allows some electricity to move through it

turbine: a machine with blades that converts the energy from a moving gas or fluid, such as water, into mechanical energy

unreliable: offering performance that is inconsistent and undependable

LERNER

SOURCE

Expand learning beyond the printed book. Download free, complementary educational resources for this book from our website, www.lerneresource.com.

Learn More about Solar Energy

Books

Bailey, Gerry. *Out of Energy.* New York: Gareth Stevens, 2011. Learn more about alternatives to fossil fuels, from geothermal to solar, and find out how you can use energy more efficiently.

Doeden, Matt. *Finding Out about Coal, Oil, and Natural Gas.* Minneapolis: Lerner Publications, 2015. Fossil fuels remain our main source of energy. Learn more about how they form, how they're collected, and the pros and cons of using them.

Waxman, Laura Hamilton. *The Sun.* Minneapolis: Lerner Publications, 2010. Take a closer look at our solar system's biggest power plant, the sun. Learn how our local star uses nuclear fusion to produce the energy that powers our planet.

Websites

Energy Kids—Solar
http://www.eia.gov/kids/energy.cfm?page=solar_home-basics
This page on solar energy includes diagrams, maps, and photos to teach you more about solar energy.

How Solar Cells Work
http://www.howstuffworks.com/environmental/energy/solar-cell.htm
Want to learn more about how a solar cell produces electricity? Check out this site to discover the ins and outs of solar cells.

Planets for Kids—the Sun
http://www.planetsforkids.org/star-sun.html
Check out this site for tons of fun facts about our sun.

Student's Guide to Global Climate Change—Solar Energy
http://www.epa.gov/climatestudents/solutions/technologies/solar.html
How do we use the energy from the sun? Check out the text and diagrams on this site to get a better idea.

Index

Photo Acknowledgments

The images in this book are used with the permission of: © Comstock Images, p. 4; © Liligraphie/Dreamstime.com, p. 5; NASA/SDO/AIA, p. 6; NASA/Goddard, p. 7; NASA/SDO, p. 8; © iStockphoto.com/daneger, p. 9; © iStockphoto.com/Hydromet, p. 10; © Jim West/imagebroker/CORBIS, p. 11; © iStockphoto.com/LongHa2006, p. 12; Dennis Schroeder/Department of Energy/National Renewable Energy Laboratory, pp. 13, 20; © Laura Westlund/Independent Picture Service, p. 14; © iStockphoto.com/sdart, p. 15; Sandia National Laboratory/Department of Energy/National Renewable Energy Laboratory, pp. 16, 29; © Tangencial/Dreamstime.com, p. 17; David Hicks/Department of Energy/National Renewable Energy Laboratory, p. 18; SkyFuel Inc./Department of Energy/National Renewable Energy Laboratory, p. 19; © Gemphotography/Dreamstime.com, p. 21; © iStockphoto.com/Sportstock, p. 22; © iStockphoto.com/da-kuk, p. 23; USDA Photo by Bob Nichols, p. 24; Aspen Skiing Co./Department of Energy/National Renewable Energy Laboratory, p. 25; SEMATECH/Department of Energy/National Renewable Energy Laboratory, p. 26; RALF HIRSCHBERGER/EPA/Newscom, p. 27; © iStockphoto.com/Elenathewise, p. 28; © Americanspirit/Dreamstime.com, p. 30; © Daniel Schoenen/image/imagebroker.net/SuperStock, p. 31; © iStockphoto.com/gmalandra, p. 32; Sacramento Municipal Utility District/US Department of Energy, p. 33; © Edmund Holt/Dreamstime.com, p. 34; © Nikolay Kazachek/Dreamstime.com, p. 35; © iStockphoto.com/Rafael Pacheco, p. 36.

Front cover: © iStockphoto.com/danielschoenen.

Main body text set in Adrianna Regular 14/20
Typeface provided by Chank